All praises belong to the Almighty

New Methods of Painting

TARIQUL ISLAM

Year 2017

Dedicated to my Dearest Mom Mrs ZINNAT ISLAM

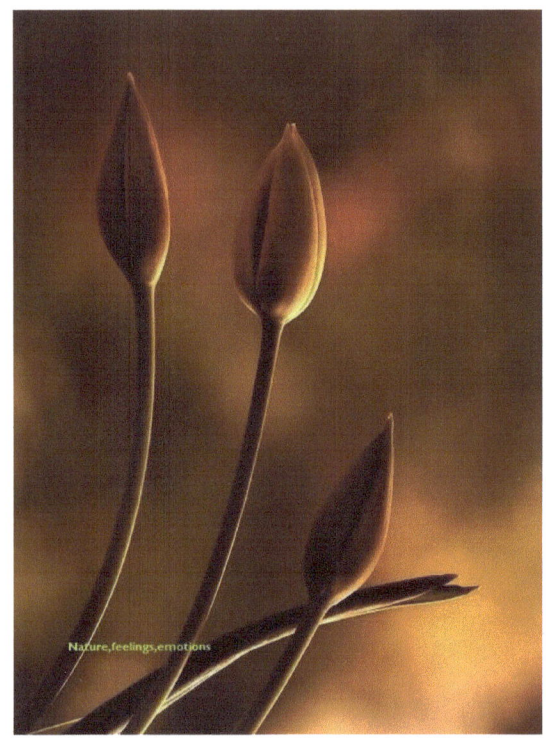

Contact: taariq2535@yahoo.com, taariqislam@gmail.com

Preface

All praises belong to the Almighty.

This book is about some new methods of painting invented by me.

Thank you.

Regards,

Tariqul Islam

TARIQUL ISLAM

April, 2017.

About me in short

I am grateful to the Almighty for all of my achievements in my life. I am a physician (MBBS) and have specialization in public health (MIPH- University of Sydney, Australia and MPH- University of New Castle, USA) and microbiology (MS in Microbiology from Stamford University Bangladesh).

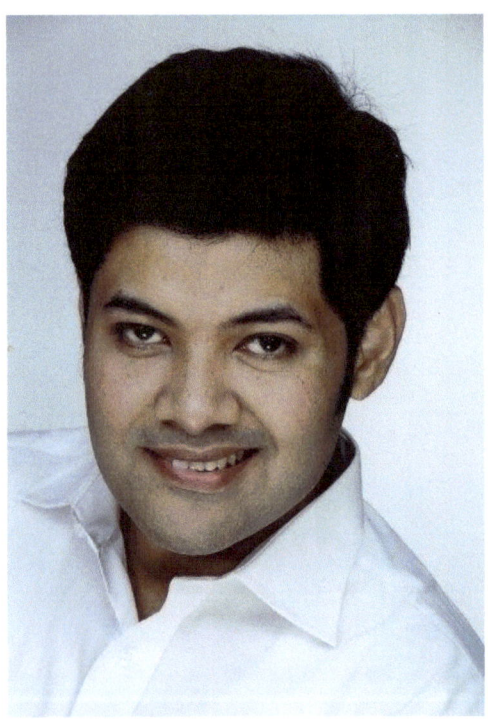

My first primary school is Saint Mary's School, Chittagong. I was the first boy in the school. Our Head Mistress's name was Mrs Rosaline Pineru. I stood third at primary talent pool examination. I studied there from class one to five. Then I studied for one year at Chittagong Collegiate School and again I was the first boy in my class. From class seven to twelve, I studied at Faujdarhat Cadet College, Chittagong. I passed MBBS in 2000 from Dinajpur Medical College under Rajshahi University of Bangladesh. I did my post graduation in Public Health as Master of Public Health from University of New Castle, USA and Master of International Public Health from the University of Sydney, Australia which is 37th ranked University of the World according to QS ranking of 2014-2015.

I also did MS in Microbiology from Stamford University of Bangladesh with the CGPA 3.98 out of 4.

By the grace of the Almighty, my 63 authored books on various subjects are available worldwide through more than 100 international networks including amazon.com, Amazon Europe, Amazon Canada and E-bay.com.

You can see my all books through the following link:

http://www.amazon.com/s/ref=nb_sb_noss_1?url=search-alias%3Daps&field-keywords=dr+tariqul+islam

You can see my author page at the following link:

http://www.amazon.com/Tariqul-Islam/e/B00BBVPBTC

or, www.amazon.com/author/tariqulislam

By the grace of the Almighty, my **200 paintings** are available at touchtalent.com and they are most popular in India, Bangladesh, Nepal, France and Poland. They are being viewed and appreciated by the artists and people of 192 countries. The link is as follows:

http://www.touchtalent.com/artist/24020/taariq-islam

My songs link:

www.soundcloud.com/islam-taariq

songs done:

1. Dil ke asmaan pe—singer-Taariq, music composition: R D Burman, remake composition: Raja Bashir

2. Jab hum jawa honge—singer- Taariq, music composition: R D Burman, remake composition: Raja Bashir

3. Dil deta hai—singer- Taariq, music composition: Anu Malik, remake composition: Raja Bashir

I am also an actor and film maker.

New Methods of Painting

TARIQUL ISLAM

Love is blind, love is a light
Love is a miracle, love is a sight

Hate is a fire, came from hatred
Hate ignites burning of a desire

Give light to love
Give sight to love

This earthy life is short
Remember that always.

TARIQUL ISLAM

Introduction

I learned to draw and paint since my childhood.

I have an online painting gallery:

www.touchtalent.com/artist/24020/taariq-islam

You can see there my many paintings and drawings.

Usually I love to draw in realistic way.

I always try to give a feeling in my drawings and paintings, I think, this is very important.

When a viewer sees any painting or drawing, he/she should feel it. It is the criteria of a good painting according to me.

Some New Methods of Art (described by painter "Taariq")

Types of paintings according to use of light/illumination:

A. Port-Ray Vision:

When an artwork or painting shows that lights/lighting are coming out from the artwork, it is called 'Port Ray Vision'.

In this painting, when you see that, you will feel a brighter lighting.

A glow of lighting you can feel in this painting.

B. Blind Vision:

When a painting shows darkness, it is called blind vision.

You will find lack of lighting in this type of painting.

Usually gloominess, sadness, night conditions are described in this type of painting.

C. Normal Vision:

When a painting shows normal illumination, it is called Normal Vision.

Usually to describe morning daylight, this type of vision is used.

D. BLACK HOLE Vision:

When there is light/illumination at only one side and other sides are dark in a painting, it is called BLACK HOLE VISION.

CRITERIA OF A GOOD PAINTING according to TAARIQ:

1. Should create a feeling in the mind of a viewer.

2. Should be understandable.

3. Appropriate way to express any object.

4. Should not be vulgar.

5. Usually related to the real world or direct from fantasy.

6. Can follow different style like realistic style, geometrical style, pot painting style, cave painting style and many more.

7. Good color combination.

CRITERIA OF A BAD PAINTING according to TAARIQ:

1. Not understandable.

2. Does not create any feeling.

3. Color combination is not good.

4. No particular style.

5. Incomplete.

6. Vulgar expression or any expression harmful for the society.

My painting History:

I was brilliant in academics since my childhood. My teachers used to love me and sometimes they used to tell others to follow me.

Usually I was very quite in my childhood and used to do all things what my parents told me.

I used to draw on walls when I was child, that time may be I was 4-5 years old. One day, our neighbor Mr Hashi Chakraborty, who was the Principal of Chittagong Art College came at our home and saw my drawing on the wall.

He told my dad, 'Who did this?'

My dad told my name and Hashi said,' I think, he will draw well. Send him to the nearest art school named Fulki.'

Then I was sent to Fulki art school and there I learned to draw and paint from professional artists like Mr Achinta and others. Mr Achinta was the regular art teacher there.

He taught us how to draw an object perfectly. He taught us how to make water color paintings. I used to go there for 3-4 years. After that I was very busy in my school education. But besides my academic career I continued my drawing and painting. When I got any leisure time, I used to draw and paint. My Mom used to keep my all drawings and paintings in a trunk.

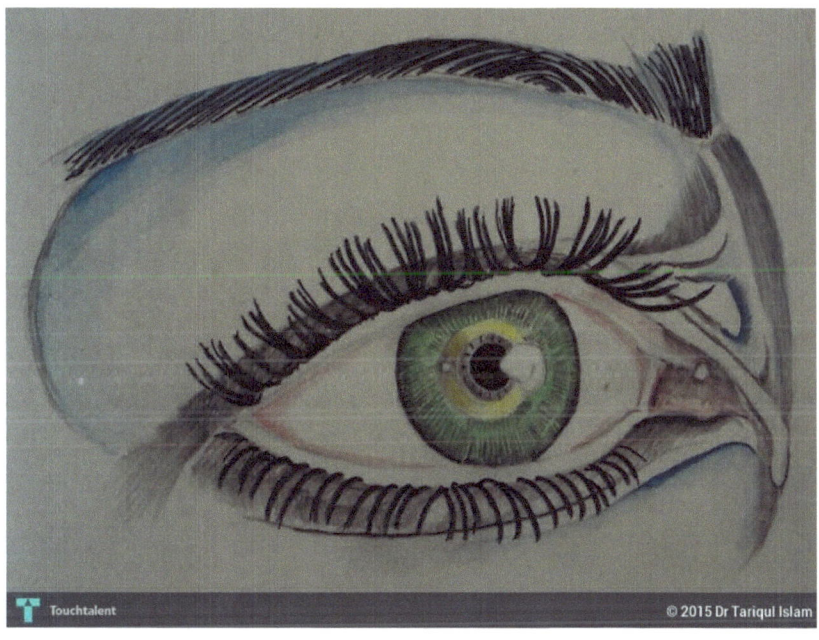

My drawing: The Eye

By the grace of Almighty, I became a physician (MBBS) from Bangladesh and after that I completed three masters successfully, two in public health and one in microbiology. I did master of international public health from the University of Sydney, Australia.

I used to read biographies of great persons. I wrote also a book on great painters like Michelangelo, Leonardo da Vinci, Rafael and Zainul Abedin. These four artists influenced me much.

I always wanted to be an exceptional, extra-ordinary person since my childhood.

I used to sing well since my childhood. My father used to sing at radio. He used to tell me and other brother to sing. Usually I could easy sing a song, but my brother could not. Then my dad used to tell me, 'Your ear is good.' It means when a person can perfectly hear a song with its every works, then he/she can sing perfectly. It is a criteria of a good singer.

Almighty gave me an extra-ordinary, melodious singing voice. So that I used to sing at stage competitions, functions at my colleges. I was serious about it in 2015. In 2016, I recorded my three songs at studio of famous singer Sir Bashir Ahmed. His son Mr Raja Bashir arranged music for me and those three songs (I think) were very nice.

I wrote already 63 books and all were published and available worldwide. This is my 64th book.

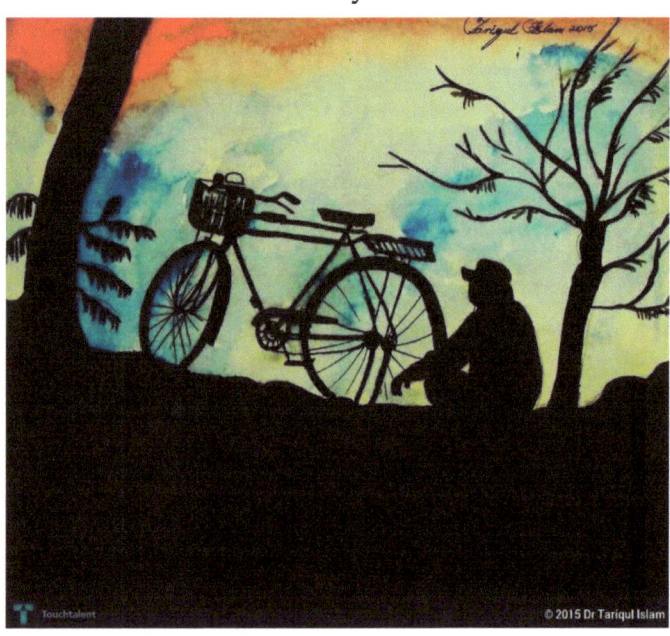

My painting: Loneliness

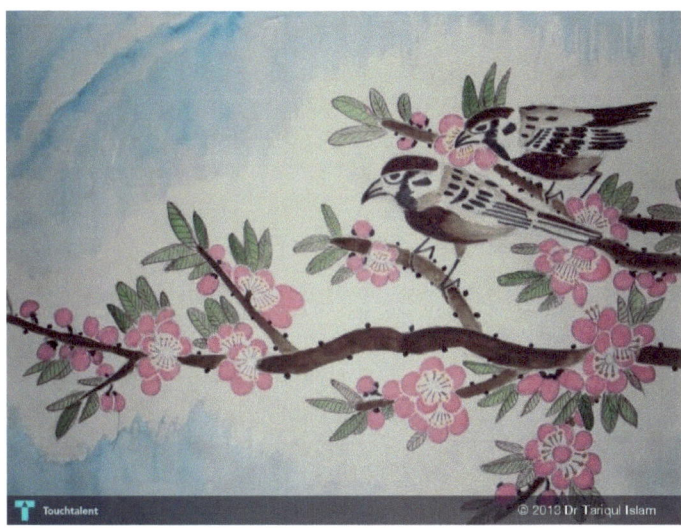

My painting: Birds and flowers

My three passions are: painting, singing and writing. Now I am also a physician and public health consultant.

I also want to do some good films where I will act. I acted at some stage dramas. Now I am taking this seriously.

If you want to be a good painter and if you are already a good painter, don't abandon this habit.

Some of my friends—I know that they are professional good painters, but they did not continue this for their jobs.

It's true, you need to be work hard for your passion.

You cannot think about every good thing with earning money.

A good painting can create an awesome impact on the mind of people.

So, go for it.

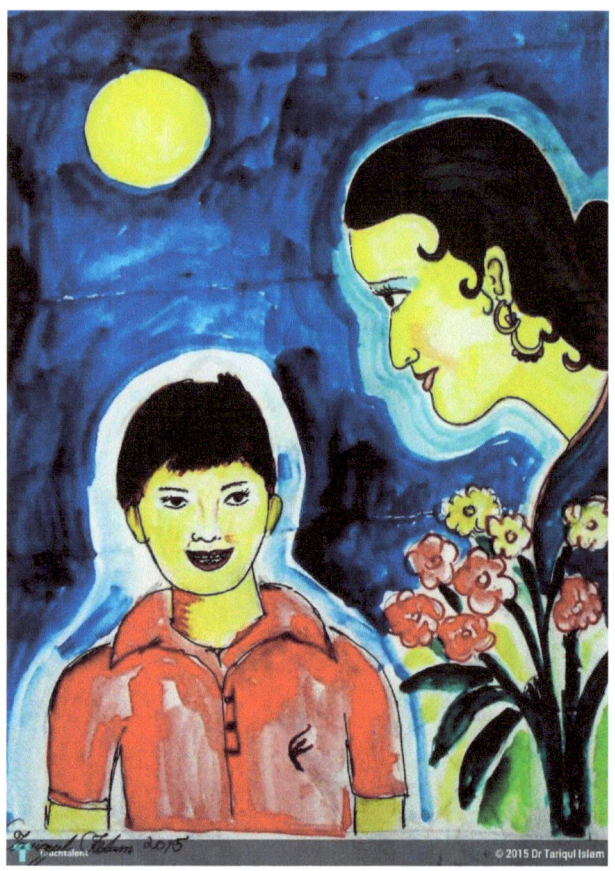

My painting: Me & My Mom

See this painting—I think this painting have unique expression. It shows the deepest love between a mother and his son. No other things are comparable with this wonderful expression. This is my view.

So, try to give an expression in your art and paintings. Don't only copy your drawings from others. This painting I made from my imagination and my love for my mother. She was just like this when she was young.

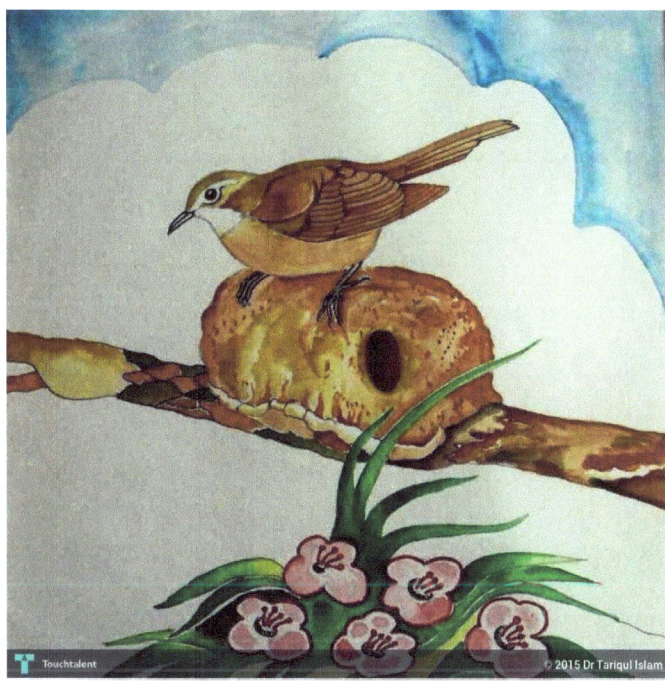

My painting: Rufouse Oven-bird

In this painting also I used my own imagination especially for the flowers.

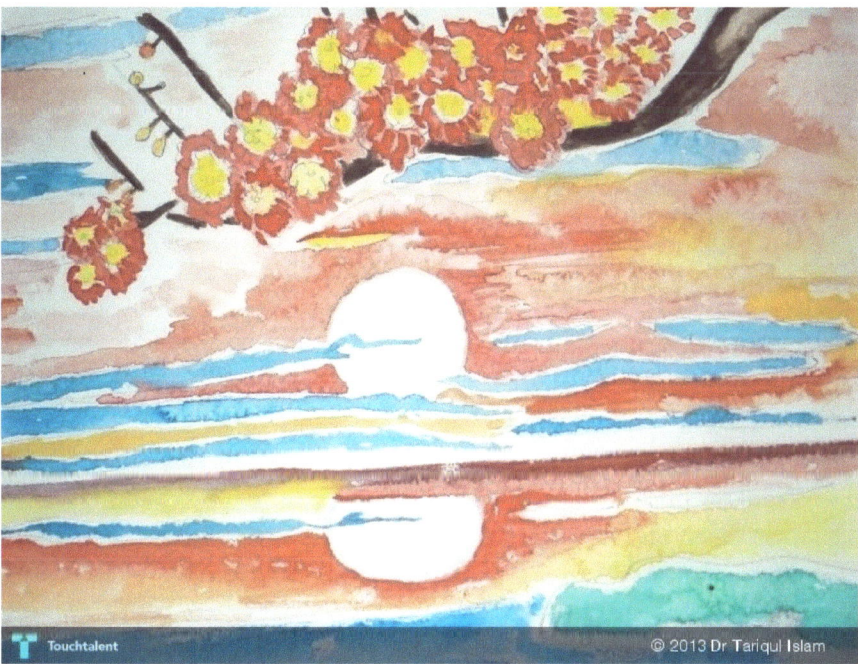

My painting: Sunset

My painting 'sunset' is one of the most viewed paintings of mine. I don't know why it suddenly attracts many people. Within a night its viewers became more than 250. May be the combination of this painting attracted the viewers.

Since 2012, I started to organize my all paintings, drawings since my childhood and did some more paintings in the year 2013 and 2014. I am grateful to my Mom that she kept my all paintings together at one place in a trunk. I then uploaded my all drawings at touchtalent.com. It actually gave a big platform for the artists to show their creativity to the world.

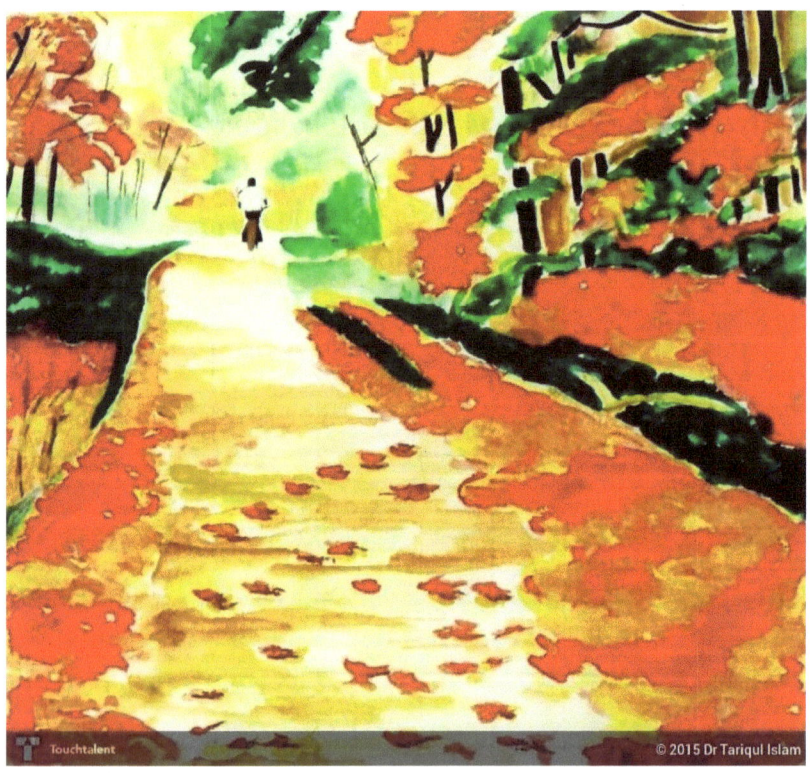

My painting- The Spring

I like this painting due to its style.

I observed that artist like Mr Zainul Abedin created his own unique style after drawing for many days. At first his drawing was like others in his initial days, then his drawing became more mature and unique.

So, if you draw for many days, you can make your own style and that is your sign or signature.

As for example, the great singer Lata Mangeshkar sang for more than 70 years in her life and still she is singing. When you hear her early songs, you cannot recognize her voice, her voice was similar to other singers, but gradually day after day, by lots of practicing she created a unique style of singing. That is her signature, her uniqueness. I like her songs very much.

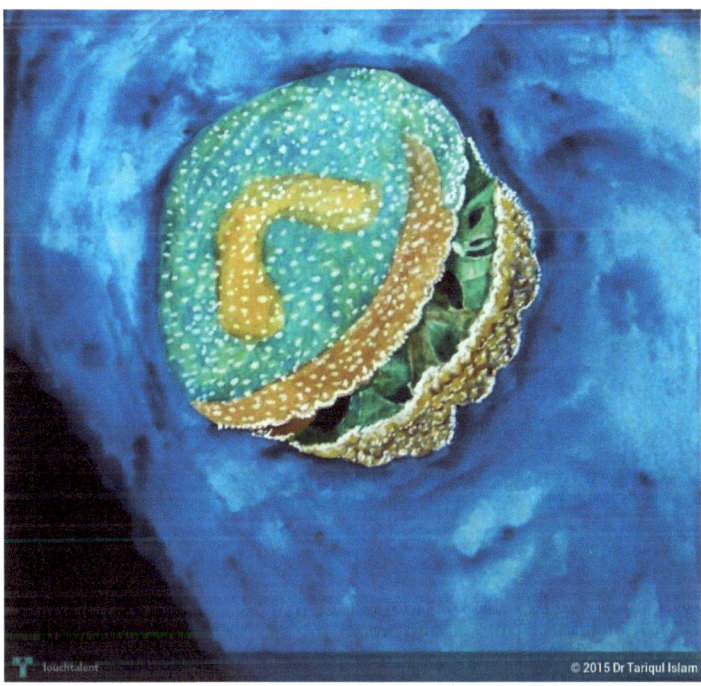

My painting: The Medusa

This painting is my favorite. It is a painting of an octopus under water. See how beautiful it looks under water.

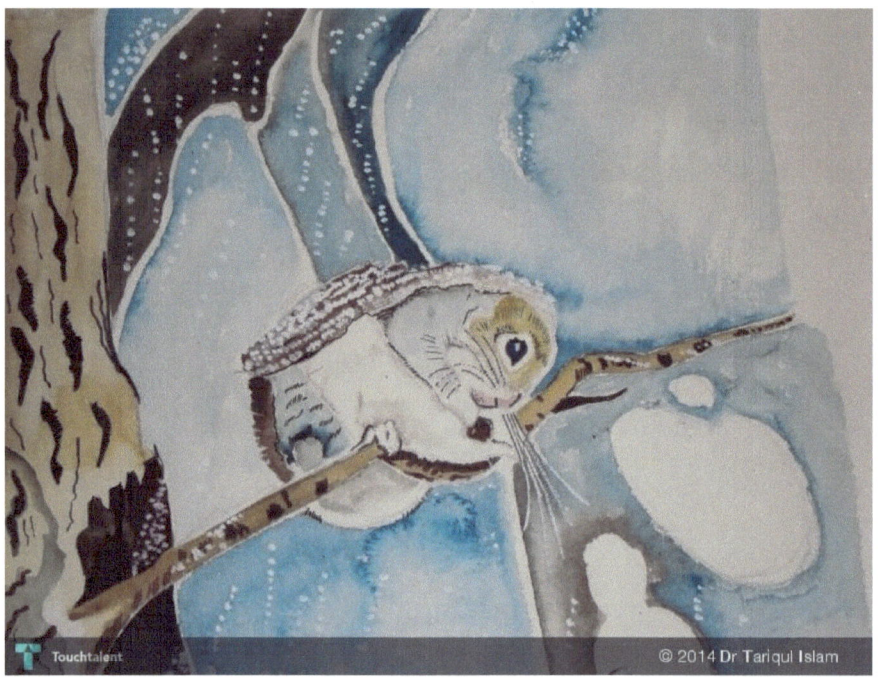

My painting: Shelter

This is one of my most viewed and appreciated paintings round the world. A small creature took shelter on the branch of a tree during snow-fall. I like its expression, probably my viewers also.

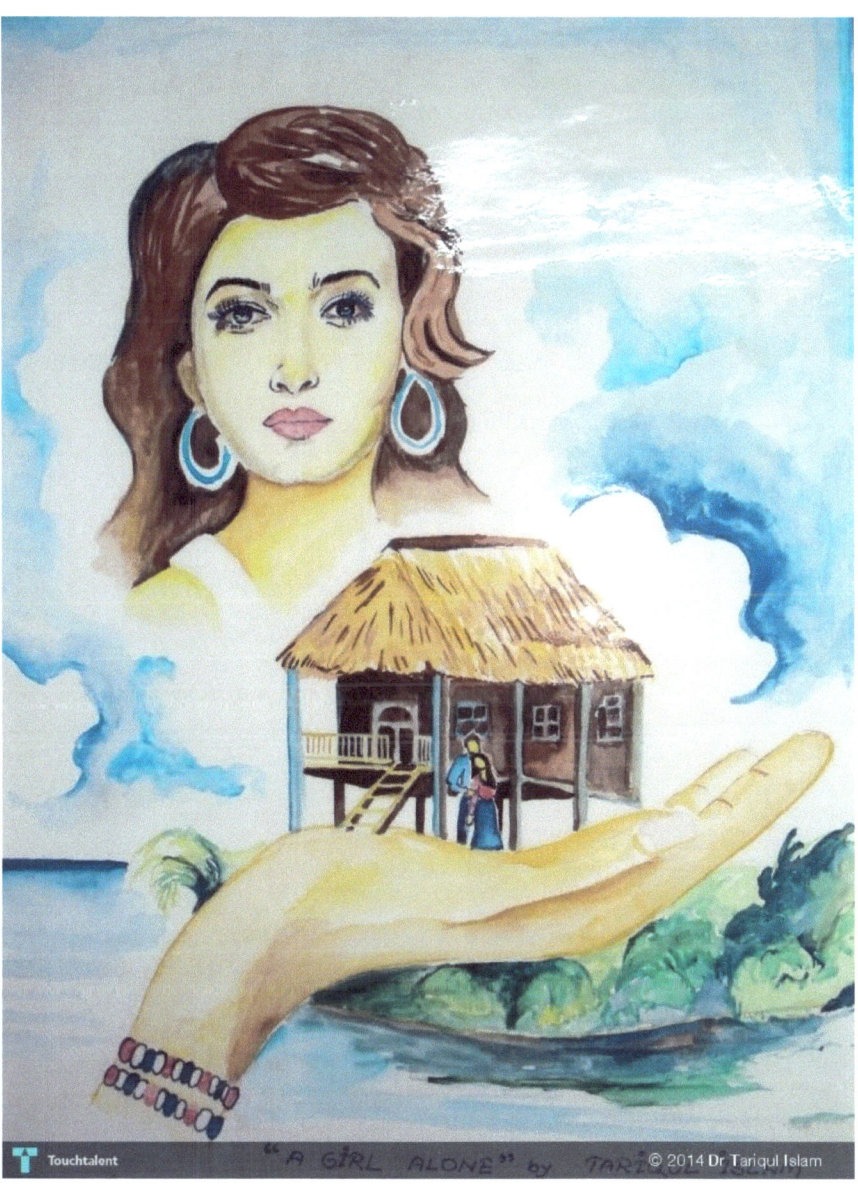

My painting: A Girl Alone.

I did this when I was a student at medical college. This is one of my favorite paintings. This painting actually tells a story. A lady is remembering her past beautiful days. This painting had participated at an international art exhibition in 2013.

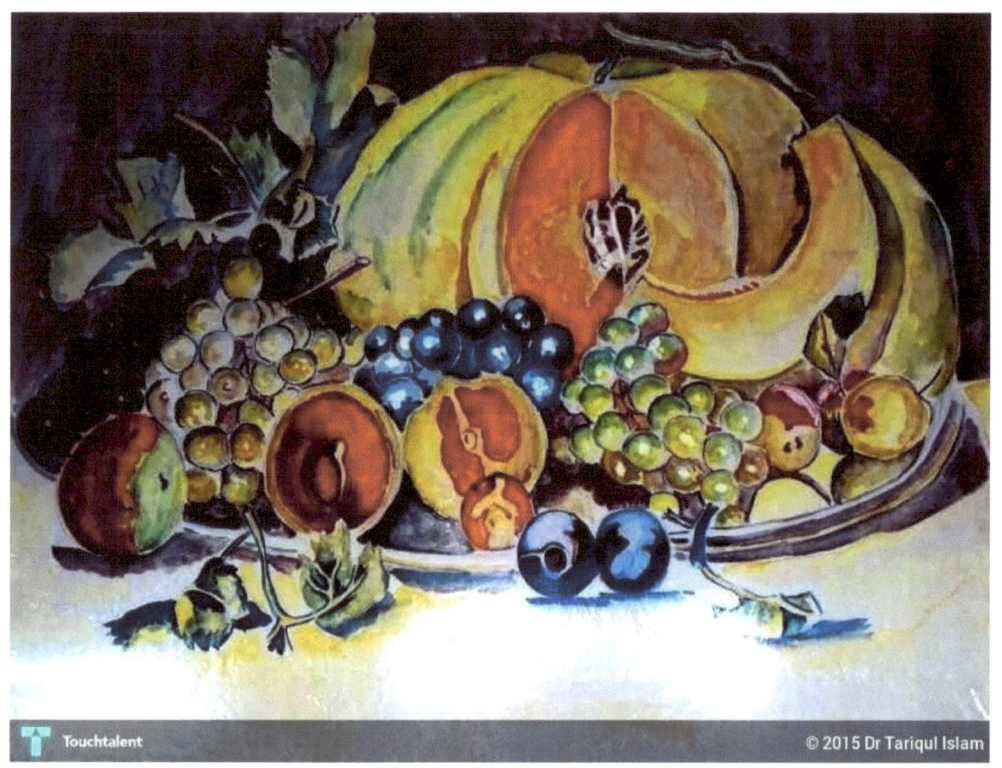

My painting: Fruits

This is also my favorite painting. I did this when I was in child.

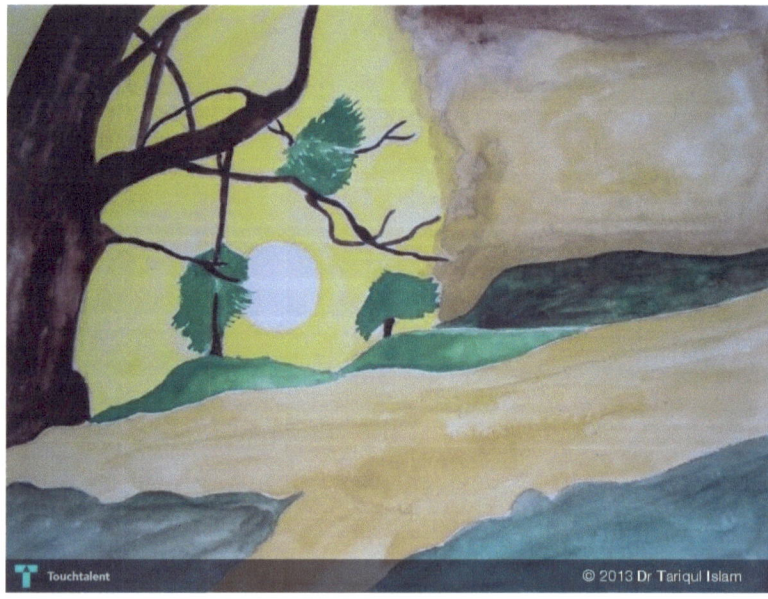

My painting: Nature

From my paintings, actually I like most the landscapes. My paintings are mostly landscape, only some are portraits.

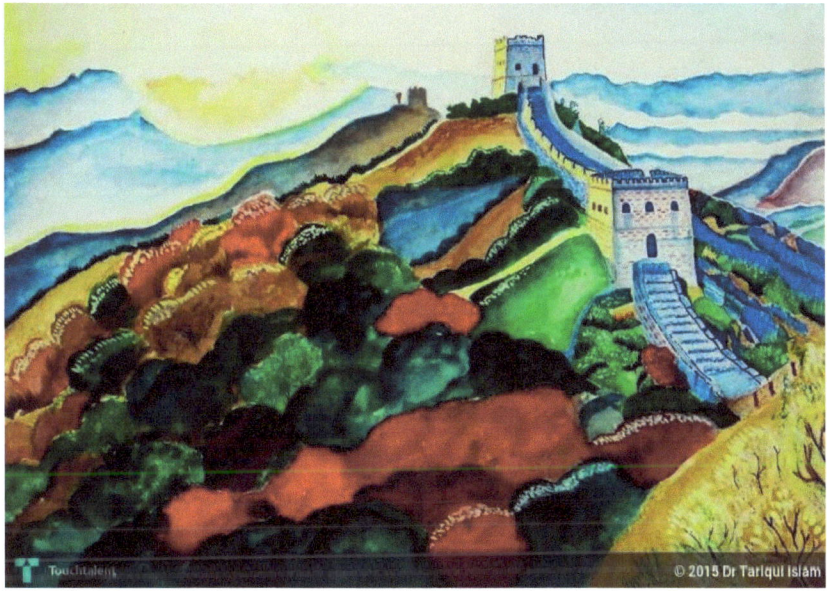

My painting: The Great Wall of China

It is also my favorite painting. In a morning, beautiful sunlight are spotting over the wall and the color of nature like blue, green and red increases its beauty.

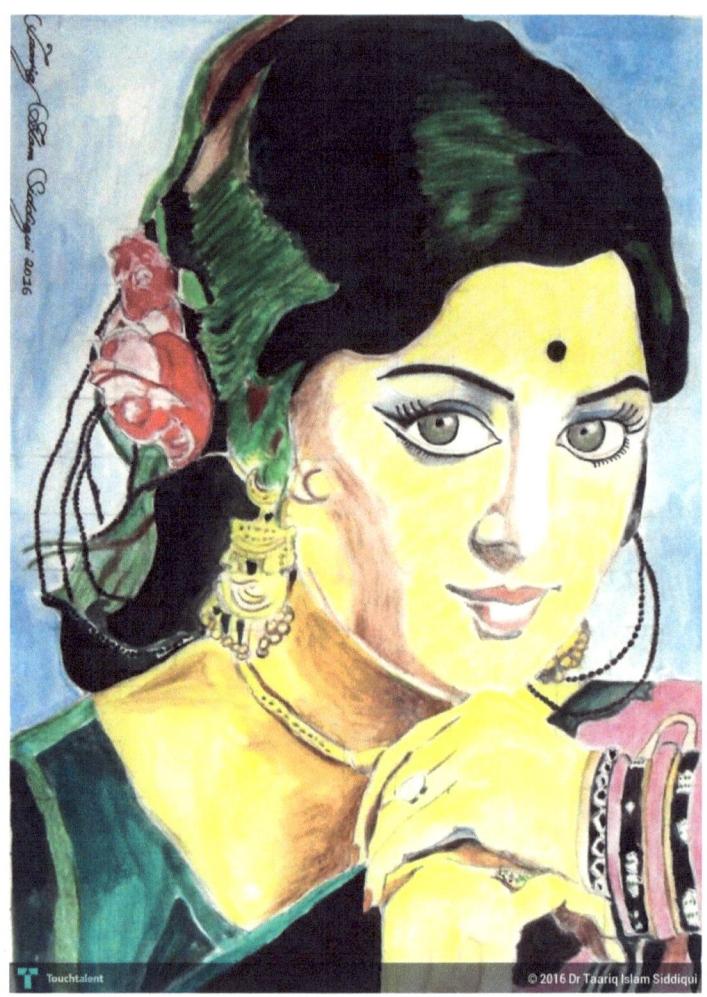

My painting: Hema Malini

This is one of my appreciated paintings.

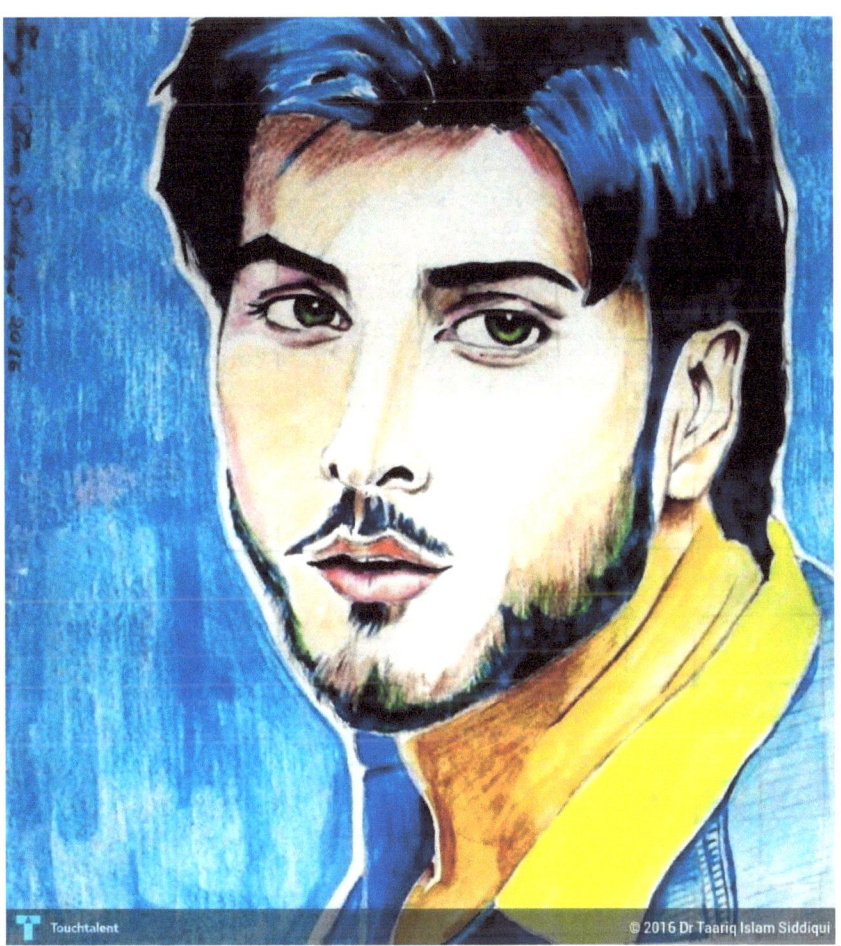

My painting: The most beautiful male of current world- Imran Abbas

This is also my favorite painting. I like his expression through eyes, hair style everything.

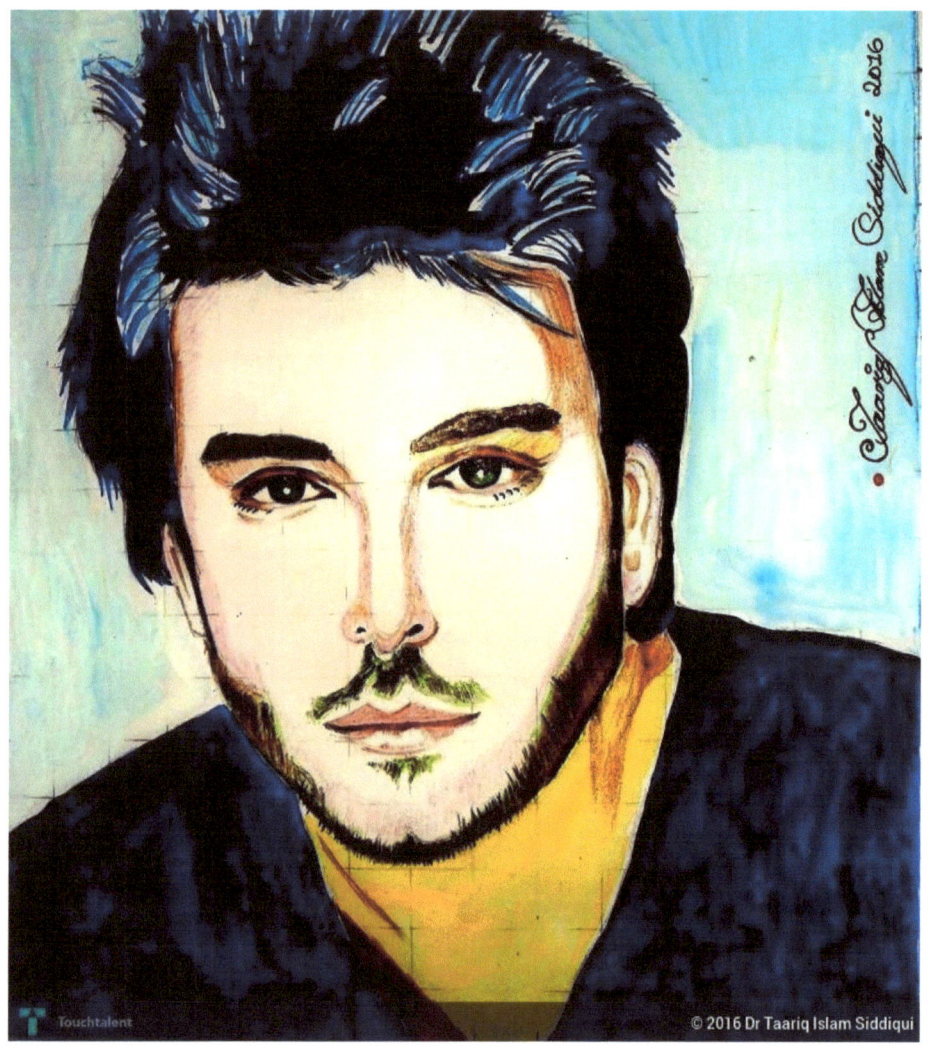

My painting: Ice-Blue Imran Abbas.

This is my favorite painting and one of my most appreciated paintings.

I especially like here the unique hair style which is very exceptional.

Thank you so much.

THE END